First published in Great Britain in 1998
by Macdonald Young Books
Reprinted in 2000 and 2004 by Hodder Wayland,
an imprint of Hodder Children's Books
Reprinted in 2007 (twice) by Wayland,
an imprint of Hachette Children's Books

This edition published in 2008 by Wayland

Reprinted in 2009

Wayland
338 Euston Road, London NW1 3BH

Printed in China

ISBN 978 0 7502 5428 1

Wayland is a division of Hachette Children's Books,
an Hachette Livre UK Company

The Story of
the Great Fire
of London

Jill Atkins

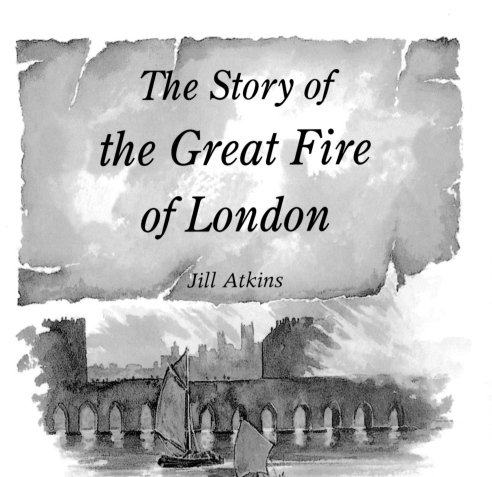

Illustrated by Julia Pearson

WAYLAND

CHRONOLOGY OF
THE GREAT FIRE OF LONDON, 1666

Sunday, September 2nd
Fire breaks out in the King's baker's house in Pudding Lane. People begin fleeing from their homes. The fire spreads quickly in the strong easterly wind.

Monday, September 3rd
Houses are pulled down in the path of the fire. The fire still spreads very fast. Hundreds of people flee, carrying what they can. The King's brother, the Duke of York, takes charge to try and keep order. Eight fire-fighting posts are set up, manned by soldiers.

Tuesday, September 4th
St Paul's Cathedral burns. Soldiers begin blowing up houses near the Tower of London. The fire is halted in that direction. The homeless people sleep in fields outside the city.

Wednesday, September 5th
The wind dies down. Soldiers blow up many houses to create big fire-breaks. The King and Duke of York help organise chains of people with buckets of water.

Thursday, September 6th
The raging fire is out, but many buildings smoulder. Soldiers continue to work to prevent it recurring. The King orders that the homeless people are fed.

Friday, September 7th
The work of clearing away the piles of burned buildings begins.

CHAPTER 1
SEPTEMBER 2ND, 1666,
LONDON
THE EARLY HOURS OF THE MORNING

William Turner sat up in bed. Something had woken him. He listened, his heart thumping. Then he heard a sound, in the distance at first, getting closer.

"Fire!" The shout came from right below William's window.

It was pitch black inside the room. William climbed out of bed and padded barefoot towards the window. He flung it open and leaned out. The smell of smoke wafted to him. He could hear lots of voices. There was a faint crackling noise too.

His brother, Thomas, came and stood beside him.

"What's happening?" he asked sleepily.

"Something big is on fire!" said William.

Through the dark narrow streets they could see hundreds of people running. Some were swinging lanterns in front of them to show them the way. Others were stumbling blindly in their panic.

"Fire!" Their voices sounded desperate to William.

"Where?" he shouted, but no one heard him or noticed him up there in the shadows.

Other people were beginning to wake up. Doors were opening and people were spilling out into the street. William saw his father down below.

"Where's the fire?" he heard him shout.

"Down by the river," cried a man. "I've heard it started in the King's baker's house in Pudding Lane.
It's spreading fast."

"What can we do?" asked Mr Turner.
"Run for your lives!" cried the man.

William shivered. Could the fire spread this far? Were they in danger?

He looked towards the river. There was a faint glow in the night sky.

Just then they heard his father close the door and come upstairs.

"Come on," William whispered to Thomas. "Don't wake the others."

They tiptoed to their parent's room and found their father already getting dressed.

"I'm going to find out for myself what's happening," he said.

"Can I come with you?" asked William.

"All right," said his father, "but Thomas is too young. He'll have to stay at home."

CHAPTER 2
THE FIRST SIGHT
OF THE FIRE

There was a faint streak of light in the sky as they set off. William could see the tall shapes of the houses towering above him on both sides of the narrow street. He couldn't imagine them burning.

It was hard keeping up with his father's enormous strides and he was soon out of breath.

"Father," he
panted, "where
are we going?"
"Up Tower
Hill. We'll have
a good view
from there."

The smell of smoke was growing
stronger. William felt it catch in the back
of his throat. It made him cough.

The view from the top of the hill made William gasp. Dozens of houses were ablaze. Bright red and orange flames were leaping into the morning sky, licking round the roofs of the wooden houses like a hoard of hungry dragons. The air was full of flying sparks and there was a crackling sound of burning wood. Clouds of thick black smoke billowed high above the flames.

Suddenly, they saw someone staggering towards them from the direction of the fire. His face was blackened and his clothes were torn and scorched.

"My home. Burned to the ground. Three hundred houses in one night."

"Did anyone try to put the fire out?" asked Mr Turner.

"No," said the man. "It took everyone by surprise. We were all in bed asleep when it started. We didn't think it would spread so fast. But there's a strong wind fanning the flames."

"We've had no rain this summer," said Mr Turner. "The houses must be tinder dry."

"I stayed in my house until the last minute," said the man, "then the fire was upon us."

He buried his head in his hands and wept loudly. William had never seen a grown man cry before. He didn't know what to do.

"Has anyone been hurt or killed?" his father asked as he sat him down on a stone wall.

The man raised his tear-smeared face.

"Not that I have heard," he said, "but hundreds of people have fled."

William felt a cold sweat sweep over him. He thought of their home, his mother, his little brothers and sisters.

"Will the fire reach our house, father?" he asked.

"I hope not, but we must return home with all haste," said Mr Turner. "If the wind changes direction, it may be upon us before another day is out."

CHAPTER 3
ESCAPE

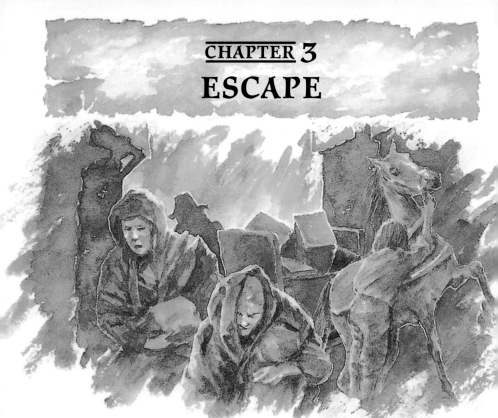

The streets were full of fleeing people, some carrying their children and possessions, others pushing hand carts piled high with furniture and boxes. Everyone was hurrying.

William clung tightly to his father's arm as they were pushed and tussled. The force of the crowd terrified him. It was like the flow of a river in flood.

When they arrived home, William's cousins were there with his aunt and uncle. His aunt looked as if she had been crying.

"We escaped only just in time," she said. "We've lost everything."

"I'm taking the family to relatives in the country," said his uncle.

"Can't anyone put the fire out?" asked William.

"Nothing works," said his uncle.
"Even King Charles himself cannot do it.
He ordered houses to be pulled down
ahead of the fire, to break its path. I saw
the soldiers carrying out his orders, but
the fire was too quick. They had to run
for their lives."

"Can't they use water from the river to put it out?" William asked.

"They've tried, but pails of water are not sufficient. I've heard that Mr Keeling's fire engines are hopelessly inadequate."

William gritted his teeth. He felt angry. Why couldn't they do something to stop the fire? At this rate it would burn its way across the whole of London until there was nothing of the city left.

When his aunt and uncle had gone he went to look for his mother. He found her upstairs with Jane, the maid, packing clothes and linen into large trunks.

"William," said his mother. "Will you do something for me? You'll have to be very brave."

William looked eagerly at his mother.

"I want you to take the little ones to your grandparents in Bethnal Green. The fire will never reach there so you'll be safe."

William didn't know whether to feel flattered or disappointed. He was pleased that his mother trusted him with the safety of his brothers and sisters. But, in Bethnal Green, he would have no way of knowing what was happening.

"Yes, mother," he said, but a plan was already beginning to form in his head.

CHAPTER 4
THE JOURNEY TO
BETHNAL GREEN

It was late afternoon by the time they set off for Bethnal Green.

"Stay close together," said Mrs Turner, "and do as William says."

"Yes, mother," they all said. But when William stepped out into the crowded streets again, he realised with horror how easy it would be to lose them.

"Lead the way," he said to Thomas and Sarah. "Keep Bessy with you. Hold each other's hands tightly."

William followed, carrying Samuel. They pushed their way amongst the people, dodging the heavy carts and keeping well clear of the horses that threatened to trample them.

"I'm tired,"
Bessy grizzled.
"I want a rest."

But it was impossible to stop. They were jostled along by the crowds. Every nerve in William's body was alert to the dangers around him. What would happen if one of them fell over? Supposing they got separated? What if the fire spread further and faster than people had thought? There was no time to think of his plan.

"We must reach Grandmother's before dark," he said.

At last the familiar tall green hedge loomed up in front of them. They ran up the path and banged on the front door.

"Thank goodness you're safe," said Grandfather when the maid had let them in. "We heard about the fire. William, come and tell me about it."

"You must all have something to eat," said Grandmother.

William was starving, but he told his Grandfather about everything that had happened. He felt very tired, too, but he did not allow himself to relax. The day was not over yet. Not by a long way. He knew exactly what he was going to do.

Thomas and Sarah were climbing the stairs when William left his Grandfather's study. Bessy and Samuel were already fast asleep.

"There's food in the kitchen," Grandmother said.

William hurried to the kitchen. He knew that what he was about to do would anger his parents, but he had done what his mother had asked. She hadn't told him what to do *after* he had delivered his brothers and sisters.

There was no time to lose. He had a long refreshing drink of water, stuffed a lump of cheese in his mouth, filled his pockets with bread and apples, and slipped out of the back door.

CHAPTER 5
THE HEAT OF THE FIRE

"What's the meaning of this?" William's father towered over him, anger in his eyes. "What are you doing here?"

William swallowed hard.

"I had to come back, Father," he said. "I want to help put out the fire."

"Can't you see how foolish you've been?" said Mr Turner. "Your grandparents will be worried about you. You could have been trampled to death, or even found yourself in the midst of the fire."

William shuddered at the memory of the terrifying journey back home. It had been almost impossible to get through. The streets were crammed with people surging in the opposite direction. Their eyes were full of fear. No one cared about him. They were all so desperate to escape the fire.

The next morning his father looked very tired. William guessed he had not slept.

"I'm going to take my boat up the river," said Mr Turner. "Are you coming?"

William ran downstairs, pleased that his father seemed to have forgiven him. A few minutes later, they were hurrying towards the river where Mr Turner's boat was moored. They clambered aboard.

As the boat approached London Bridge, William stared, horrified at what he saw. Houses on the bridge were burning fiercely, as the fire swept across the city, devouring everything in its path. The noise was deafening. Amongst the thick black smoke and the roaring and crackling of the fire, people were yelling and screaming. In blind panic, they clung to boats and jetties, or flung themselves into the river.

As soon as the boat reached the
burning bridge, Mr Turner leapt onto it.
"Come on William," he shouted.
"We must get these people to safety."

All through that day and into the
night they struggled to rescue people.
William was totally exhausted, but
somehow he kept going.

"I hope our house is all right," he
shouted above the roar of the flames.

His father nodded. "If the wind
changes direction we'll be homeless
like all of these people."

It was just getting light when William felt a fresh wind on his cheeks.

"Quick!" shouted his father. "We must go home and save our possessions."

CHAPTER 6
EXPLOSIONS!

When William and his father arrived home they found that his mother and Jane were no longer in the house.

"They must have gone to your grandparents," Mr Turner said. "The fire could reach here very soon."

William felt sick. Would their house really burn down?

"I need your help," said Mr Turner.
William followed him out into the
garden where they dug a deep pit.

"What's this for?" William asked.

"You'll see."

William helped carry boxes of wine
and cheese and some important papers
out to the garden. They lowered them
into the pit.

"At least these will be safe from the
fire," said Mr Turner.

They had just finished filling the pit when someone thundered on the door.

"Run!" a voice shouted. "The fire has reached the Dolphin Tavern."

"That's only two streets away," said William.

Carrying what they could, they joined the crowds fleeing from the fire.

"Where are we going?" William asked.
"To your grandparents," said his father.
 "Will anyone ever stop the fire?"
Suddenly, a loud explosion rocked the
ground beneath William's feet.
He screamed and dived underneath a
cart. He hit the ground hard but he did
not notice.

"What was that?" His voice was shaking as much as his body was.

Another explosion shook the ground. William put his hands over his ears.

A patrol of soldiers came round the corner.

"Clear the street," the officer commanded. "The King has ordered us to blow up houses in the path of the fire."

They ran into a house and William and his father hurried away. A third explosion roared behind them.

William was so exhausted that he fell asleep as soon as they reached his grandparents. Overnight, news came that the explosions were finally succeeding. The fire was beginning to die down.

CHAPTER 7
OUT AT LAST!

Blackened skeletons of houses stood
silhouetted against the clear, bright
morning sky. Everywhere lay silent
under a coating of fine grey ash. Smoke
wafted upwards in places where the fire
still smouldered. The smell of charred
wood was strong.

News had travelled fast. The fire that had raged for four days and nights was out. William and his father walked briskly through the streets. William was thinking about their house. It had been his home all his life. He was trying hard not to cry.

"Will our house be like this?" he asked.

Mr Turner did not answer. His eyes were staring straight ahead and his mouth was set in a grim hard line. William had never seen his father look like that before. He took hold of his arm and saw his face relax.

They hurried on, past the burned-out shell of the Dolphin Tavern. William felt his father shudder as they approached the corner of their street.

They stopped. William stared. He couldn't quite believe it. The fire had got no further than the houses that the soldiers had blown up. The King's orders had worked. Their house was safe! William found he was crying. His father hugged him.

"Let's hurry back to your grandparents' house and tell them the good news," he said.

William's feet hardly touched the ground as they hurried to Bethnal Green.

"The fire's out!" he shouted as they arrived. "Our house is safe!"

"You were foolish to run off alone at night," said Grandfather as they sat at dinner.

"I'm sorry," said William.

His father stood up. "I've already scolded him," he said. "Now it's time to thank him." He turned to William.

William smiled. He felt warm and happy. It was good to be praised! It was also good to know that the Great Fire of London was out…

INTERESTING FACTS

Bethnal Green
In 1666 this was a village in countryside outside London. Now it is part of London itself.

The City of London
At the time of the Fire the population of London was about 400,000. The fire destroyed approximately 13,000 houses (about one fifth of the total houses), St Paul's Cathedral, 87 churches and many important buildings. About 200,000 people were made homeless by the fire but very few people were killed. When the Fire was over, the King asked Sir Christopher Wren, the famous architect, to help rebuild the city. Houses were built in brick instead of wood. Wren designed the new St Paul's Cathedral and many other beautiful churches and buildings all over London. Although many of his churches were destroyed by German bombs in World War II, some can still be seen today.

John Keeling's Fire Engine
This had a very weak pumping system that needed several men to make it work. Its hoses were not flexible and so it was difficult to direct the water. After the Great Fire, insurance companies were set up and formed their own fire brigades, but it was not until 1829 that steam-powered pumps made fire-fighting much more effective.

King Charles II (1630-85)
After the execution of King Charles I in 1649, Oliver Cromwell took over the government of the country. Charles II was forced to spend many years in exile. After Cromwell's death, Charles returned to England and became king in 1660.

London Bridge
This was badly burned, but not destroyed in the fire, although many of the buildings on it were. A new bridge, built in 1823-31, is now in Arizona, USA. The present London Bridge was built in 1967-72.

Samuel Pepys (1633-1703)
This man wrote a very famous diary. In it there is a detailed description of the Great Fire.

Pudding Lane
You can still visit the place where the fire started. A monument was erected here on the site of the baker's shop near the River Thames.

Tower Hill
This is next to the Tower of London. Many executions took place here, as well as in the Tower.